~~Off~~ with
her head!

Off with her head!

ENGLISH HERITAGE

First published in Great Britain in 2007 by
English Heritage • Kemble Drive • Swindon SN2 2GZ

Packaged by Susanna Geoghegan
Text copyright © Complete Editions

ISBN 9781905624508

Printed in China by Hung Hing

Introduction

Henry VIII is one of the most colourful and controversial monarchs in English history. Famous for his six wives and his enormous girth in later life, he is probably its best-known king.

During his reign, England began to flex its muscles on the world stage. It turned from being a Roman Catholic country, which owed spiritual loyalty to the pope in Rome, to an independent Protestant country, in which the sovereign was head of the church in England – where, for the first time, it became lawful to read the Bible in English. At the same time Henry VIII promoted English independence by laying the foundations of a powerful navy, to enforce English control of the high seas and protect its growing maritime trade, and fortified the coastline to guard his island stronghold from invasion. Wales was legally annexed to England, wars were fought and won against Scotland and France, and Henry became the first English monarch to call himself king of Ireland. Across the Atlantic, exploration of the New World began and men of vision and imagination started to understand that many ideas about the world that had been accepted since ancient times were fundamentally wrong.

Meanwhile, the English Reformation, as this period of enormous change became known, encouraged an atmosphere of enquiry and learning. The writing and teaching of celebrated scholars and philosophers spread new thought and culture. From Europe came the great teachings of the Dutch scholar, Erasmus; at home, men like Sir Thomas More, who served Henry as lord chancellor, encouraged a new humanist way of seeing the world and mankind's role in it. The whole system of education was reformed, setting down the foundations for the flowering of English culture two generations later under Henry's youngest daughter, the future Queen Elizabeth I.

For all the forward thinking that characterised his reign, however, Henry VIII retained much of the prejudice and self-interest of the medieval kings who had gone before him. Fundamental to these was his obsession with maintaining the Tudor dynasty, founded by his father Henry VII.

Off with her head!

3

Put simply, Henry VIII wanted a son to succeed him and ensure that the Tudor royal line would be maintained – and he moved heaven and earth (almost literally in his break with the Church of Rome) to make this happen. In his drive to achieve this ambition, wives were married and discarded, loyal statesmen were executed, holy scripture was quoted and then ignored. And the two daughters born to his first two wives were largely sidelined. One of the great ironies of English history is that the second of these, Princess Elizabeth, grew to become one of the most influential English women of all time and one of her nation's greatest sovereigns.

She is one of the many fascinating characters to feature in her father's story, which began full of hope and promise when he became England's dashingly good-looking young king in April 1509. But the country's best-known king had not been brought up to rule his father's realm. Henry was the second son and when he was born in 1491 his older brother Arthur, Prince of Wales, was set to ascend to the throne; young Prince Henry, therefore, was educated to go into the church. But then, not for the last time in English history, the heir to the throne died, changing Henry's destiny and the destiny of the country for ever. Shortly after becoming king he married his brother's widow, the Spanish princess Catherine of Aragon.

Their marriage began happily and survived the loss of a baby son, who died a week after his birth in 1511; five years later their only surviving child, a girl named Mary, was born. As Queen Catherine grew older, though, the chances of her producing another living son began to ebb away and by 1526 the king's interest was directed elsewhere, towards a 20-year-old lady of the court named Anne Boleyn.

Henry had already taken her sister, Mary, to be his mistress. But Anne held out against following her into the king's bed until she could do so as his wife. Henry became infatuated by her and the only solution to his dilemma was to divorce Catherine. In achieving this he was helped by Cardinal Thomas Wolsey, an ambitious and gifted politician who rose to become lord chancellor, the most important man in England after the king. It was Wolsey who suggested to Henry that the death of his and Catherine's children might be a direct sign that their marriage was not blessed in the eyes of God, even if the pope had sanctioned it.

Henry latched on to this eagerly and instructed Wolsey to petition Pope Clement VIII to annul his marriage to Catherine. However, international power politics intervened. The negotiations dragged on, trying the king's patience as his ardour for Anne Boleyn grew. In the end his patience snapped. He turned on Wolsey, deprived him of his office and stripped him of his wealth. Broken in spirit and health, the great cardinal was dead within a year.

In his place Henry had appointed as his chancellor Sir Thomas More, whose conversation and erudition fascinated him. But More was a man of principle, as the king would discover. In January 1533 Henry secretly married Anne Boleyn, after eight learned institutions, both on the continent and at home, agreed with the king that the laws of God forbade a man from marrying his brother's widow. In other words, the pope had been wrong to allow his first marriage, and Henry regarded himself free to dispose of Catherine and make Anne his legal wife.

Off with her head!

Of course, this also meant that there was no chance of receiving the pope's blessing, and drastic action would follow. Sir Thomas More could see the way things were heading and resigned his office in 1532, to be replaced by Thomas Cromwell who had previously worked as Wolsey's secretary. Working with the Archbishop of Canterbury, Thomas Cranmer, and urged on by the king, Cromwell drew up legislation in 1533 and 1534 which severed England from the power of the pope, so that Henry could declare himself Supreme Head of the Church of England.

Through this Henry gained more than a seductive young wife; power over the church placed at his mercy the vast wealth accumulated by England's great religious houses over the centuries; nothing and no one would stand in the way of his plunder. Sir Thomas More was one of many who refused to accept the king's newly acquired authority; all were executed. Throughout the second half of the 1530s the 600 or more monasteries, abbeys and convents in England were systematically dismantled, with their property passing into the hands of the king and his nobles.

However, the lack of a male heir remained a problem. Anne had given birth to another daughter, Elizabeth, but this left Henry no better off than he had been with Catherine of Aragon. After three years of marriage, Anne Boleyn was charged with a series of monstrous crimes and swiftly executed.

Off with her head!

For Henry VIII, it was to be third time lucky. Jane Seymour, the daughter of Sir John Seymour, who had served as lady in waiting to both of Henry's former wives, succeeded Anne as queen and at last gave birth to a boy, Edward, but his mother did not survive beyond the first days of his life. Henry was genuinely distraught and, in the words of one commentator, 'continued a widower two years after'.

Now it was the turn of Thomas Cromwell to try his luck in the international marriage market. Cromwell was eager to establish close links with other European Protestants and suggested that the German princess, Anne of Cleves, might provide a suitable catalyst to achieve this. Unfortunately the portrait of her that persuaded the king to agree to the marriage flattered the lady more than a little. Henry was appalled when he saw his future wife in person and wasted little time in having the marriage annulled and Anne of Cleves pensioned off.

Next in line was pretty, perky Catherine Howard, the cousin of Anne Boleyn and a member of the family which stood at the head of English Catholic nobility. She lasted two years as Henry VIII's fifth wife, before he discovered that she had been unfaithful and promptly had her executed.

Finally, in 1543, the bloated, irritable old man – so different to the handsome young prince who had married Catherine of Aragon – took another Catherine, Catherine Parr, as his sixth and final wife. With her he saw out his closing years, which ended in January 1547.

A tyrant and a ruthless despot he may have been, but Henry VIII was also a shrewd judge of the nation he ruled over. In the eyes of his subjects, he tied his own destiny to the fate of the country as a whole. This may have allowed him greater freedom than similar dictators, but Henry VIII was careful never to push his advantage too far. There were uprisings during his reign, but his dynasty set down strong roots, endured through three more reigns and survives in the national memory as probably the most formative in the history of England.

Accession Hopes

Henry VIII ascended the throne of England in a fanfare of promise and eager expectation. Many commentators (like Lord Montjoy, here writing in a letter to the celebrated Dutch scholar Erasmus) saw him as the ideal of a Renaissance prince: a scholar, soldier, statesman and, in his youth, an outstanding sportsman.

'What may you not promise yourself from a prince with whose extra-ordinary and almost divine character you are acquainted? When you know what a hero he now shows himself, how wisely he behaves, what a lover he is of justice and goodness, what affection he bears to the learned, I will venture to swear you will need no wings to make fly to behold this new and auspicious star!

If you could see how here all the world is rejoicing in the possession of so great a prince, how his life is all their desire, you could not contain your tears for sheer joy. The heavens laugh, the earth exults … Avarice is expelled from the country, extortion is put down, liberality scatters riches with a bountiful hand. Yet our King does not desire gold, gems or precious metals, but virtue, glory, immortality!'

According to Luther

The example of Henry VIII was not universally admired. 'A pig, an ass, a dunghill,' Martin Luther once remarked of him, 'the spawn of an adder, a basilisk, a lying buffoon, a mad fool with a frothy mouth.'

A-Hunting We Will Go

Like many early Tudor gentlemen, Henry VIII was passionate about hunting. The excitement of the chase was one thing, but hunting had other qualities that appealed to him. As he commented somewhat pretentiously as a young man: hunting was a way to avoid 'idleness the ground of all vyce and to exercise that thing that shal be honourable and to the bodye healthfull and profitable'.

Alas, What Shall I Do For Love?

Henry VIII was an accomplished musician and composer. Although it is doubtful that he composed the quintessentially English song, known by its shortened title 'Greensleeves', which became closely associated with him, over 30 compositions have been acknowledged as Henry's own work, of which this is one.

> *Alas, what shall I do for love?*
> *For love, alas, what shall I do?*
> *Since now so kind*
> *I do you find*
> *To kepe you me unto.*
> *Alasse!*

Anxieties of an Expectant Father

Writing to the Duke of Norfolk, during the time of Jane Seymour's confinement, Henry expressed his worries about not travelling too far from her until the baby [the future Prince Edward] was born.

'... being but a woman, upon some sudden and displeasant rumours and bruits that might by foolish or light persons be blown abroad in our absence, being specially so far from her, she might take to her stomach such impressions as might engender no little danger or displeasure to the infant with which she is now pregnant (which God forbid!), it hath been thought by our council very necessary that, for avoiding such perils, we should not extend our progress further from her than sixty miles.'

An Apple a Day

Henry VIII was very partial to fruit and ensured that the royal orchards and gardens were well stocked with apples, plums, damsons, cherries and strawberries (the last being particular favourites of his). Following his marriage to Catherine of Aragon he developed a strong liking for oranges, which were costly and rare in 16th-century England, as they were imported from Spain. Later in his reign Henry introduced apricots into England, establishing them in the gardens of Nonsuch.

Arms and the Man

In 1513 English armies achieved their greatest victories during Henry VIII's reign. The king himself led an army across the Channel to wage war in France and captured two French towns. Meanwhile, with Queen Catherine left to rule the country in his place, another army marched north and inflicted a crushing defeat on the Scottish army led by James IV, who was killed at Flodden Field along with 10,000 of his countrymen. Writing in his *Chronicle*, Charles Wriothesley recorded these notable events:

'This year also, on the day of the Exaltation of the Cross, *Te Deum* was sung in St Paul's Church for the victory of the Scottish field, where King James of Scotland was slain. The King of England that time lying siege before Tournai in France, and won it and Tourraine also.'

The Art of Diplomacy

When Henry VIII enlisted a certain nobleman to serve as his ambassador to King Francis I of France, the newly appointed delegate was anything but pleased, since relations between the two countries were at a dangerously low ebb.

One day, having taken down a particularly aggressive message which Henry wanted him to relay to the French king, the ambassador begged to be excused on the grounds that the hot-tempered Francis might have him executed for daring to deliver such a missive.

Henry reassured him, explaining that if Francis killed him there were dozens of Frenchmen in England whose heads Henry could chop off in revenge.

'But of all these heads,' the ambassador ruefully remarked, 'there may not be one to fit my shoulders.'

Attending the King's Pleasure

Having to endure two years of stalemate over Henry VIII's divorce from Catherine of Aragon did not appeal to Anne Boleyn, who once complained, 'I have been waiting long and might in the meanwhile have contracted some advantageous marriage, out of which I might have had issue, which is the greatest consolation in this world. But alas! Farewell to my time and youth spent to no purpose at all.'

An Audience with the King

'We at length reached the King, who was under a canopy of cloth of gold, embroidered in Florence, the most costly thing I have ever witnessed. He was leaning against his gilt throne, on which there was a large gold brocade cushion, where the long gold sword of state lay. He wore a cap of crimson velvet, in the French fashion, and the brim was looped up all around with lacets, which had gold enamelled tags. His doublet was in the Swiss fashion, striped alternately with white and crimson satin, and his hose were scarlet and slashed from the knee upwards. Very close round his neck he had a gold collar, from which there hung a round cut diamond, the size of the largest walnut I ever saw, and to this was suspended a most beautiful and very large round pearl. His mantle was of purple velvet, lined with white satin, the sleeves being open, and with a train verily more than four Venetian yards in length.

This mantle was girt in front like a gown, with a thick gold cord, from which there hung large glands entirely of gold, like those suspended from the cardinals' hats; over his mantle was a very handsome gold collar, with a pendant St George, entirely of diamonds. On his left shoulder was the garter, which is a cincture buckled circular-wise, and bearing in its centre a cross gules on a field argent; and on his right shoulder was a hood, with a border entirely of crimson velvet. Beneath the mantle he had a pouch of cloth of gold, which covered a dagger and his fingers were one mass of jewelled rings.'

The Venetian ambassador, describing his audience with Henry VIII on 23 April, 1515

Between a Rock and a Hard Place

As her marriage to Henry VIII fell apart, Catherine of Aragon found increasing solace in her religious faith. Her daughter, Princess Mary, could not escape her mother's religious fervour. The pressure on her was intensified when her father demanded that she accept the Act of Succession, which would have meant Mary publicly acknowledging that her parents' marriage was invalid and that she was therefore illegitimate. Meanwhile, her mother was urging her that to agree to Henry's demands would be to offend God.

Early in 1534, after Henry had married Anne Boleyn, Mary received this letter from her mother and the tension she was under must have increased even more. It goes a long way towards accounting for the unhappiness and emotional insecurity Mary suffered throughout her life:

'Daughter, I heard such tidings today that I do perceive if it be true, the time is come that Almighty God will prove you; and I am very glad of it, for I trust He doth handle you with a good love. I beseech you agree of His pleasure with a merry heart; and be sure that, without fail, He will not suffer you to perish if you beware to offend Him. I pray you, good daughter, to offer yourself to Him. If any pangs come to you, shrive yourself; first make you clean; take heed of His commandments, and keep them as near as He will give you grace to do, for then you are sure armed … [obey] the King, your father, in everything, save only that you will not offend God and lose your own soul; and go no further with learning and disputation in the matter.'

Bewitching and Bewitched

'… a beauty not so whitely as clear and fresh above all we may esteem … There was found, indeed, upon the side of her nail upon one of her fingers some little show of a nail, which yet was so small by the report of those that have seen her, as the work-master seemed to leave it an occasion of greater grace to her hand, which, with the tip of the one of her other fingers, might be and was usually by her hidden.'

George Wyatt, *Extracts from the Life of Queen Anne Boleigne*, first printed in 1817. All this tortuous sentence amounts to is that Anne Boleyn had the beginnings of an extra finger on her left hand – a fact that led a number of her enemies to label her as a witch.

Birthday Greetings

After Jane Seymour had given birth to Henry VIII's son, Prince Edward, 2,000 guns were fired from the Tower of London in the celebrations that followed.

Blighted in the Eyes of God

When it became evident that Catherine of Aragon was incapable of bearing a son and heir, Henry VIII became obsessed with the text in Leviticus which stated, 'If a man shall take his brother's wife it is an unclean thing … they shall be childless.'

This was one of the principal grounds for his seeking an annulment of the marriage.

Calculations of a Queen-in-Waiting

'For something like five years she [Anne Boleyn] succeeded in holding him [Henry VIII] at arms' length, a remarkable performance, all things considered, and probably indicative that there was considerably more of cold calculation than of passion in Anne's attitude.'

Conyers Read, *The Tudors*

Camelot Revisited

The legend of King Arthur had a profound effect on several English kings. Edward III built a circular banqueting hall to hold a round table and formed the Order of the Garter to include the most valiant knights of his day, both of which evoked the celebrated Round Table of Arthurian myths.

Henry VIII went one better, however, and had his own face painted on Arthur's image on the table.

Cap of Maintenance

The only surviving article of clothing known to have been worn by Henry VIII is a cap of maintenance, which was presented to the mayor of Waterford in 1536.

A cap of maintenance is a crimson velvet cap, lined with ermine, which serves as one of the insignia of the British sovereign. It is paraded directly before the sovereign on state occasions, such as the State Opening of Parliament. King Henry's cap of maintenance is housed in the Waterford Museum of Treasures.

Cardinal Sins

Born the son of an Ipswich butcher, Thomas (later Cardinal) Wolsey rose to become the most powerful man in the country, second only to King Henry himself. However, Wolsey rapidly shook off his humble origins and displayed the worst excesses of power, privilege and wealth in his dealings with others, as described here.

'And after mass he would return to his privy chamber again, and being advertised of … noblemen and gentlemen, and other persons, would issue out into them, apparelled all in red, in the habit of a cardinal; which was either of fine scarlet, or else of crimson satin. Taffety, damask, or caffa, the best he could get for the money; … he had also a tippet of fine sables about his neck; holding in his hand a very fair orange, whereof the meat or substance within was taken out, and filled up again with the part of a sponge, wherein was vinegar, and other confections against the pestilent airs; to the which he most commonly smelt unto, passing among the press, or else when he was pestered with many suitors.'

George Cavendish, *The Life and Death of Thomas Wolsey*, 1667. Cavendish, who was in constant attendance on Wolsey as his usher, was also his first biographer.

Child Protection

The birth of a surviving male heir had cost Henry VIII three marriages, a break with the Roman Catholic Church and the enmity of Catholic rulers throughout Europe. So ensuring Prince Edward's well-being as a baby was of paramount importance – and the king was diligent in safeguarding his infant son.

The baby's quarters were equipped with their own kitchen, where his food could be prepared in complete safety; even so every dish had to be tasted before being given to the king's son. No food or unwashed crockery or kitchen utensils were to be left lying around where they might attract flies or vermin. The king decreed that all floors and walls in the vicinity of the prince's apartments had to be scrubbed with soap and water three times a day. The same standards of hygiene were required of anyone coming into contact with the royal baby. No one in his household was permitted to speak to anyone suspected of being in contact with the plague and none of them were allowed to visit London during the summer without permission, for fear that they might act as carriers of the deadly infection. Illness was not the king's only concern for his son; assassination was a constant worry and even dukes were required to obtain written authority from the king himself before approaching the little prince in his cradle.

Chimes and Alarums

Among Henry VIII's most treasured possessions were his clocks – objects of great expense and technical accomplishment which, in the 16th century, were the exclusive preserve of only the very wealthy. Henry's collection included 17 standing clocks with chimes and 'alarums'; 'a hanging clock enclosed in glass with plummets of lead and metal'; maritime ones which showed 'how the sea doth ebb and flow'; and calendar clocks that displayed 'all the days of the year with the planets, with three moving dials'. A royal horologist was paid 40 shillings a year to maintain this prized collection of timepieces.

Chivalry and Combat

All the pageantry and chivalry of the high Middle Ages were still alive and well during the reign of Henry VIII. Crowds of spectators attended tournaments to watch noble 'warriors' test their skill at arms. Those taking part in a tournament would enter their names on a 'Tree of Chivalry' and would process to the tiltyard, where the tournament was held, preceded by marshals of the joist and accompanied by drums and trumpets.

Lords and knights rode side by side in pairs, fully armed; behind them came 'His Majesty, armed cap-a-pie [head to foot], surrounded by 30 gentlemen on foot, dressed in velvet and satin'.

Jousts were usually held to honour ladies, who presented their chosen knights with favours, such as scarves or handkerchiefs. The winning knight received his accolade from the queen or the highest ranking lady present – and, in his younger days, the winner was not infrequently the king himself.

As a 16-year-old, Henry was said to have practised his jousting skills every day. As early as 1510 one foreign observer commented, 'There are many young men who excel in this kind of warfare, but the most conspic-uous among them all, the most assiduous and the most interested in the combats is the King himself, who never omits being present at them.'

Five years later a Venetian visitor recorded that Henry jousted 'marvel-lously'. He and his companions had been invited by the king 'to see him joust, running upwards of 30 courses, in one of which he capsized his opponent, who is the finest jouster in the kingdom, horse and all. He then took off his helmet and came under the windows where we were, and talked and laughed with us to our very great honour, and to the surprise of all beholders.'

On another occasion, Henry is recorded appearing at a tournament attired in 'cloth of gold with a raised pile', and looking 'like St George in person as he entered the lists'.

In those early years of his reign, England's young king seemed to be the very embodiment of the chivalric ideal.

Christmas at the Court of Henry VIII

In Tudor times Advent, which lasted through the first three weeks of December, was a period of penitence. When this ended on Christmas Eve, however, fasting was replaced by feasting, with celebrations that reached their climax on twelfth night (6 January) the Feast of the Epiphany. Throughout the Christmas banqueting, pageantry and general merry-making held sway, presided over by the Lord of Misrule, or Master of Merry Disports, with his retinue of heralds, magicians, and fools in fancy dress.

Henry VIII was a willing participant in all the Christmas traditions. He cheerfully accepted that for this brief period in the dead of winter rank gave way to revelry. Henry also followed the medieval custom of appointing a boy bishop to take the place of a senior chaplain; records from Windsor show that he once rewarded a boy, appropriately named Nicholas, with 10 marks for carrying out his duties as boy bishop.

Continual Festival

'Continual festival' was the way in which Catherine of Aragon described the early part of her marriage, in a letter to her father, King Ferdinand of

Spain. Edward Hall, the English chronicler of Henry's reign, confirms this in his description of the typical royal routine during a progress south and west of London in the summer of 1510, the year after Henry and Catherine were married.

According to Hall, Henry's days were busily spent, 'shooting [practising archery], singing, dancing, wrestling, casting of the bar [throwing heavy wooden or metal weights], playing at the recorder, flute, virginals, and in setting of songs, making of ballads, and did set two goodly masses, every of them five parts, which were sung oftentimes in his chapel and afterwards in divers other places. And when he came to Woking, there were kept both jousts and tournays. The rest of this progress was spent in hunting, hawking and shooting.'

Court and Social

Although her marriage to Henry VIII lasted barely six months, Anne of Cleves did not disappear entirely from the court. In addition to occasional visits as 'the king's sister', the royal style she had agreed to after the annulment of her marriage, Anne of Cleves was also present at Henry's marriage to his sixth and last wife, Catherine Parr, and at the coronation of his eldest daughter, Mary I.

A Cup Fit for a Queen

After Henry VIII had made Jane Seymour his third wife, he lavished presents on her. Hans Holbein, the king's painter, designed several magnificent pieces of jewellery which were made by the royal goldsmiths. Among these were an emerald pendant set with pearls. He also had made a huge gold cup weighing 1.85kg, lavishly decorated with the royal monogram of H & I, with his new bride's coat of arms, and the highly appropriate motto: 'Bound to serve and obey'.

Cupid and the King

Among the surviving love letters written by Henry VIII to Anne Boleyn during their courtship is this one, which shows the level of the king's infatuation:

'In debating with myself the contents of your letters I have been put to a great agony; not knowing how to understand them, whether to my disadvantage as shown in some places, or to my advantage as in others. I beseech you now with all my heart definitely to let me know your whole mind as to the love between us; for necessity compels me to plague you for a reply, having been for more than a year now struck by the dart of love, and being uncertain either of failure or of finding a place in your heart and affection …'

Dallying with Duckies

After several years of trying to seduce Anne Boleyn, Henry VIII reputedly succeeded with a saucy love letter in which he praised her breasts, or 'sweet duckies' as Henry liked to call them. These were a source of fascination for more than obvious reasons, since the object of the king's desire was said to be blessed with an extra 'duckie'.

Defence of the Realm

Faced with the prospect of invasion after his break with Rome, Henry set about fortifying the English coast. From East Anglia to Cornwall, a string of castles and gun batteries were built to fight off any attempted landings, largely paid for by the profits that came to the Crown from the dissolution of the monasteries.

Duty Calls

Henry's dismay at the physical appearance of Anne of Cleves could barely be disguised. On his wedding day he told Lord Chancellor Cranmer, 'My Lord, if it were not to satisfy the world, and my Realm, I would not do that I must do this day for one earthly thing.'

Dying for the Faith

By the mid-1540s Catherine Parr's interest in theology had almost certainly led her to develop Protestant opinions which gained her powerful enemies at court, among them Henry's new lord chancellor, Wriothesley. In February 1546, the king was informed that the queen had been named as a Protestant sympathiser by a known Protestant woman, Anne Askew. Despite savage racking and torture in the presence of the lord chancellor, Askew refused to renounce her faith or to implicate anyone else. She was sentenced to death and burned at the stake – though for her death came quicker than it did for many. Someone had paid her executioner to hang a bag of gunpowder round her neck, so that she would be killed when this exploded rather than facing the torment of the flames.

Educating Elizabeth

Catherine Parr did much to reunite King Henry with his children. Ten-year-old princess Elizabeth in particular formed a close bond with her step-mother, who encouraged the education of this intelligent girl, who was well-versed in the classics and already spoke several languages – which was unusual for a Tudor girl, even a princess. In return, the young princess wrote many affectionate letters to Queen Catherine, signing them from 'Your Majesty's very dear Elizabeth'. When she was still only 11 years old, Elizabeth sent her stepmother the translation she had made of Queen Marguerite of Navarre's *Mirror of the Sinful Soul*. This was bound in covers beautifully embroidered by the young princess, and accompanied by a touching letter of gratitude.

English Spoken Here

The Laws in Wales Act of 1535 legally annexed Wales, joining it with England to form a single nation. If that wasn't bad enough for the people of Wales, the new laws also established English as the sole language to be used in official proceedings in Wales, to the great inconvenience of the numerous people who only spoke Welsh.

Entente Cordiale

Early in his reign Henry had led an army across the English Channel and defeated a French army at the so-called Battle of the Spurs. So relations between him and the king of France, Francis I, were understandably edgy when they met on the plain in Picardy in June 1520, at what became known as the Field of Cloth of Gold, because of the huge quantity of the precious fabric on display and the lavish and extravagant arrangements that were made for jousting, dancing and banqueting. Francis was seeking English support against Charles V, emperor of the Holy Roman Empire. Both monarchs were accompanied by magnificent retinues, all of whom were accommodated on or close to the site – the most prominent in magnificent pavilions, which included a temporary palace, others having to make do as best they could, with more than a few nobles being forced to 'lie in hay and straw'.

Some who witnessed the three-week extravaganza called it the 'eighth wonder of the world'; the cost was certainly of wondrous proportions. Henry VIII is calculated to have spent well in excess of £4,500,000 in today's money and the French were paying off their share for the next 10 years – the catering bill alone came to the equivalent of over £2,650,000. 'Never was seen in England such excess of apparelment before,' commented a bishop, outraged at the extravagance that permitted not far short of a million pounds to be spent on jousting clothes alone. Every significant member of both the French and English courts was in attendance – with their retinues an estimated 6,000 people.

For all the outward show of harmony, suspicion and tension ran through the elaborate proceedings. 'I fear the English even when they bring gifts,' Francis told Henry, only half-jokingly, while a Venetian observer noted, 'These sovereigns are not at peace. They hate each other cordially.' His remarks were prescient. No alliance was made between France and England, and within three years of the extravagant charade the two countries were at war again.

Entertaining the King

In their early days together, Henry VIII had the highest regard for Thomas Wolsey, who was indispensable to the successful administration of Henry's policies at home and abroad. The report sent to Rome when Henry was promoting Wolsey as a worthy candidate for cardinal, stated that 'the King can do nothing of the least importance without him and esteems him among the dearest friends'.

The high regard was reciprocal. Wolsey's gentleman usher and first biographer, George Cavendish, confirmed that Henry was a regular visitor to Wolsey's house and for his part Wolsey ensured that whenever the king was his guest, 'there wanted no preparations of goodly furniture, viands of the finest sort that might be provided for money or friendship.

Such pleasures were then devised for the King's comfort and consolation as might be invented or by man's wit imagined. The banquets were set forth with masque and mummeries in so gorgeous a sort and costly manner that it was heaven to behold. There wanted no dames or damsels meet or apt to dance with the maskers or to garnish the place for the time, with other goodly disports.'

Famous Last Words

'The executioner is, I believe, very expert. And my neck is very slender. Oh God have pity on my soul!'

These were words reputedly spoken by Anne Boleyn at her execution. The executioner of Calais had been brought to London to execute King Henry's ill-fated queen with a sword, according to French practice, instead of with the axe used by English executioners. Queen Anne refused the offer of a blindfold and the executioner found her so disarming that he had to get someone to distract her attention on the scaffold, so that he could steal up behind her to carry out the death penalty.

The choice of execution had been one of the last favours granted to Anne Boleyn by Henry VIII. 'The King has been good to me,' she cheerfully acknowledged. 'He promoted me from a simple maid to be a marchioness. Then he raised me to be a queen. Now he will raise me to be a martyr.'

When, as traditionally required, Anne Boleyn's executioner raised her severed head to shout 'So perish all the king's enemies!' the crowd were horrified to see that its eyes and lips continued to move.

As no one had thought to provide a coffin for her corpse, the late queen's body was bundled into a narrow chest and buried beneath the choir of the Tower church, St Peter ad Vincula, that afternoon.

Henry VIII was never again heard to mention her name.

Farewell From a First Wife

'My most dear lord, king and husband,

The hour of my death now drawing on, the tender love I owe you forceth me, my case being such, to commend myself to you, and to put you in remembrance with a few words of the health and safeguard of your soul which you ought to prefer before all worldly matters, and before the care and pampering of your body, for the which you have cast me into many calamities and yourself into many troubles. For my part, I pardon you everything, and I wish to devoutly pray God that He will pardon you also.'

The last letter from Catherine of Aragon to Henry VIII

Farewell ~~from~~ a Second Wife

'Neither did I at any time so far forget myself in my exaltation, or received queenship, but that I always looked for such alteration as now I find; for the ground of my preferment being on no surer foundation than your grace's fancy, the least alteration was fit and sufficient (I know) to draw that fancy to some other subject. You have chosen me from a low estate to be your queen and companion, far beyond my desert or desire.'

Anne Boleyn on herself, in her last letter to Henry VIII

Feast Fit ~~for~~ a King

One eyewitness account of a banquet held by Henry VIII described the mesmerising feast as follows:

'So many courses and dishes were served that for once there were too many to tell, and indeed too many for the guests. The King had ordered four courses of ten pairs of dishes in each, but thoughtfully eliminated one course of ten to reduce the time that the ambassadors would have to sit at the table. As it was, he would have had to partake of thirty pair of such dishes: roast capons and partridges, civets of hare, meat and fish aspics, lark pasties and

36

rissoles of beef marrow, black pudding and sausages, lampreys and savoury rice, entrement of swan, peacocks, bitterns and heron born on high, pasties of venison and small birds, fresh and salt water fish with gravy of shade the colour of peach blossom, white leeks and plovers, duck and roast chitterlings, stuffed pigs, eels reversed, frizzled bean, finishing off with fruit wafers, pears, comfits, medlars, peeled nuts and spiced cider.'

First Among Equals

In 1525 King Henry became the first king of England to number himself, when he styled himself Henry VIII. He was also the first English sovereign who was styled His Majesty. His father, Henry VII, had been styled His Grace and His Highness.

Fixed Ideas

Henry VIII was not a monarch who found making decisions easy. He was sometimes in the habit of mulling over an issue for longer than his advisers thought necessary. Once his mind was made up, though, it was virtually impossible to make him change it. Cardinal Wolsey knew this trait in his master's character from long experience and warned, 'Be well advised what ye put in his head, for ye shall never pull it out again.'

A Flanders Mare

In an attempt to consolidate the Protestant faith in England, Thomas Cromwell was eager to strengthen ties with Protestant realms in Europe. Since Henry VIII was in need of another wife (his fourth), Cromwell persuaded him that marrying Anne of Cleves would be an advantageous match.

The lady in question was not known to the king, so the court painter, Hans Holbein, was engaged to paint an entrancing portrait of her. This had the desired effect and the king, as hoped, looked forward to meeting his new bride with lustful anticipation.

When she finally arrived, however, the princess turned out to be rather more homely than the portrait suggested, and in his disappointment the furious king exclaimed, 'You have sent me a Flanders mare!'

Someone had to pay for the inconvenience and embarrassment caused by such a serious diplomatic blunder and, as its chief architect, Cromwell was the unfortunate scapegoat. His execution was swift in coming, when Henry was persuaded to have him executed on trumped-up charges of treason.

Flodden Field

When Henry VIII was campaigning in France, Catherine of Aragon temporarily ruled the country. Following the great victory of the English army over the Scots at Flodden, she wrote a letter to her husband, enclosing with it a piece of the coat worn by the Scottish king, James IV, who was killed in the battle. She had thought to send the dead king himself but, as she explained, 'our Englishmen's hearts would not suffer it. It should have been better for him to have been in peace than have this reward. All that God sends is for the best.'

Full Favour

'Of all the wives of King *Henry* she only had the happiness to die in his full favour, the 14th of *Octob.* 1537, and is buried in the quire of *Windsor* Chappell, the King continuing in *real mourning* for her even all the *Festival of Christmas*.'

Thomas Fuller, *The History of the Worthies of England*, describing Henry VIII's grief at the death of his third wife, Jane Seymour

Give a Dog a Bad Name

In order to marry Anne Boleyn, and hopefully sire a son to succeed him, Henry VIII asked the pope to annul his marriage to Catherine of Aragon. Cardinal Wolsey was sent to the Vatican to conduct the negotiations on behalf of the king and everything appeared to be going well, until the cardinal had kneeled in homage to kiss the pope's toe (in actual fact the cross embroidered on his right shoe). This was the moment when Wolsey's greyhound, Urian, decided to leave his own mark on the proceedings by charging forward and biting down hard on the papal foot. This injury brought the negotiations to a swift and unsatisfactory conclusion. Henry did not get the annulment to his marriage and the English Reformation followed shortly afterward.

Good and Faithful Servant

Thomas Cromwell worked single-mindedly in establishing the absolute authority of the Crown in England and in the Protestantisation of the

Church. However, his efforts won him many enemies and when he slipped in the king's favour, after negotiating Henry's disastrous marriage to Anne of Cleves, his end was quick in coming.

However, Henry's remorse at Cromwell's downfall was clear from a comment made shortly after his execution: 'On light pretexts, by false accusations, they made me put to death the most faithful servant I ever had.'

Handsome Is As Handsome Does

In his younger days Henry VIII was a strikingly good-looking young man. When he was in his mid-twenties the Venetian ambassador considered him to be, 'the handsomest potenate I have ever set eyes upon; above the usual height, with an extremely fine calf to his leg, his complexion very fair and bright, with auburn hair combed straight and short in the French fashion, and a round face so very beautiful that it would become a pretty woman, his throat being rather long and thick … He speaks French, English, and Latin, and a little Italian, plays well on the lute and harpsichord, sings from book at sight, draws the bow with greater strength than any man in England, and jousts marvellously. Believe me, he is in every respect a most accomplished Prince; and I, who have now seen all the sovereigns in Christendom, and last of all these two of France and England in such great state, might well rest content.'

Heart's Ease

After her beheading, Anne Boleyn's heart was stolen and hidden in a church near Thetford in Norfolk. It was reburied beneath the church organ in 1836.

Hell Hath No Fury ...

One version of Anne Boleyn's fall from grace suggests that Henry's attentions to Jane Seymour kindled furious jealousy in her. Anne had been married to Henry for barely two years when his interest began to shift towards the woman who would become her successor as his wife and queen.

According to one account, Jane had only recently arrived at court when Queen Anne spotted a magnificent jewel hanging round her neck and asked if she could see it. Jane Seymour blushed and drew away, but Anne snatched it violently from her. Looking at the jewel more closely she saw that it contained a miniature of Henry, which he had clearly presented to her rival.

Worse was to follow. A few days after the burial of Catherine of Aragon, Anne chanced upon Jane seated on the king's knee enjoying his caresses. Flying into another jealous rage, Anne threatened Jane with terrible revenge and ordered her from the court that instant.

Well aware that her star was rising in the king's affections while Anne's was sinking, Jane Seymour ignored her and waited for destiny to take its inevitable course – or so that particular story goes.

Holy Writ

The availability of the Bible in English was a source of division in the early years of Henry VIII's reign, when only the Latin version was sanctioned by the Church. Sir Thomas More, who succeeded Thomas Wolsey as Henry's lord chancellor, was strongly opposed to an English translation of the Bible, on the grounds that the Church alone should be responsible for the teaching and interpretation of holy scripture. An English Bible, it was argued, would allow far too many people access to its teachings which would inevitably lead to them forming their own opinions on religious matters, something the Church would never allow.

During his time in office, Sir Thomas More followed a policy of strict censorship. No books in English printed outside the country were to be imported, no matter what their subject was. Within the country itself, no books on scriptural or religious subjects were allowed to be printed unless prior permission had been granted by a bishop.

However, there was a feverish black market in Bibles and other religious books which convinced even the king that an English Bible should be permitted, and in 1536, just a year after the death of Sir Thomas More, Miles Coverdale's translation of the Bible was published with the assent of Henry VIII.

In the Bleak Mid-Winter

The weather was so cold at the beginning of 1537 that in January Henry and his queen, Jane Seymour, rode across the frozen River Thames on horseback to Greenwich Palace.

In the King's Name

When he was first crowned, Henry used the style 'Henry the Eighth, by the Grace of God, King of England, France and Lord of Ireland'. In 1521, Pope Leo X rewarded the king with the title 'Defender of the Faith', for a book he had written which attacked Martin Luther and defended Catholicism.

As a result the royal style became 'Henry the Eighth, by the Grace of God, King of England and France, Defender of the Faith and Lord of Ireland'. After the breach with Rome, Pope Paul III rescinded the grant of the title 'Defender of the Faith'. However an act of Parliament declared the title still valid so Henry continued to use it.

Further changes followed. In 1535 Henry added the 'supremacy phrase' to the royal style, which became 'Henry the Eighth, by the Grace of God, King of England and France, Defender of the Faith, Lord of Ireland and of the Church of England on Earth Supreme Head'. A year later another amendment was made, so that the phrase 'of the Church of England' became 'of the Church of England and also of Ireland'.

Judgement of History

In 2002 the BBC sponsored a poll to nominate the 100 Greatest Britons: Henry VIII was ranked 40th.

King Henry's Bounty

Henry VIII did not earn his popular nickname 'Bluff King Hal' from being picky with his food. The king had a hearty appetite to say the least, and the court dined on gargantuan feasts that became the talk of Europe.

Nowhere else in the early 16th century did people enjoy such plentiful and varied supplies of food as those consumed by English nobles.

Although laws passed in 1517 were intended to restrict the amount served at meals, the king was exempted. The quantity of food consumed by the court in a 'normal' day of feasting was prodigious. A typical inventory of ingredients passing through the royal kitchens included: 11 carcasses of beef, 6 sheep, 17 hogs and pigs, 45 dozen chickens, 15 swans, 6 cranes, 32 dozen pigeons and 54 dozen larks, 6 dozen geese and 4 peacocks. The meat and fowl required 3,000 pears and 1,300 apples to flavour and garnish their respective dishes. Royal bakers turned out 3,000 loaves of bread and the royal dairies and butteries supplied 400 dishes of fresh butter.

Set against this enormous quantity of produce is the number of diners who had to be fed. Every day between 500 and 1,000 people dined 'from King Henry's bounty' and on special occasions the numbers could rise to 1,500. As one commentator pointed out, 'Feeding them required nearly as much planning, provisioning and scheduling as feeding an army on campaign. When the vast hall or great chamber was filled for dinner or supper, and the diners removed their caps to shouts of "Room for the sewer!" as the dishes were brought in, there were nearly always more mouths to be fed than anyone had foreseen.'

Lady Friends

Only two of Henry's mistresses can be identified with certainty: Bessie Blount and Anne Boleyn's sister, Mary. Evidence suggests that he may have had affairs with a number of other women. Jane Popicourt, a Frenchwoman at the English court and a mistress of the kidnapped Duc de Longueville, may have been Henry's lover in 1510. Four years later his name was linked with Lady Anne Stafford, sister of the Duke of Buckingham and wife of Lord Hastings. Twenty years on, in 1534, Anne Boleyn's cousin, Margaret (Madge) Shelton is thought to have become Henry's mistress. There are also references from this same time to an 'unknown lady' who was enjoying her sovereign's intimate attention.

Landscape Legacy

'... Nothing can be said in his vindication, but that his abolishing of Religious Houses and leaving them to the ruinous depredations of time has been of infinite use to the landscape of England in general, which probably was a principal motive for his doing it, since otherwise why should a Man who was of no Religion himself be at so much trouble to abolish one which had for ages been established in the kingdom?'

Jane Austen, *The History of England*

Lion of England

'If a lion knew his own strength, hard were it for any man to rule him.'
Comment on Henry VIII, attributed to Sir Thomas More

The Longed-for Heir

'On 27 May 1537, Trinity Sunday, there was a *Te Deum* sung in St Paul's cathedral for joy at the queen's quickening of her child, my lord chancellor, lord privy seal and various other lords and bishops being then present; the mayor and aldermen with the best guilds of the city being there in their liveries, all giving laud and praise to God for joy about it. The bishop of Worcester, Dr Latimer, made an oration before all the lords and commons after the *Te Deum* was sung, explaining the reason for their assembly, which oration was marvellously fruitful to the hearers. And also the same night various great fires were made in London, with a hogshead of wine at every fire for the poor people to drink as long as it lasted. I pray Jesus, if it be his will, to send us a prince.'

The chronicler Edward Hall, recording the public excitement at the pending birth of Jane Seymour's baby. Hall's prayers, and those of the king and many more of his subjects, were answered in the small hours of 12 October, when she gave birth to a son: the future Edward VI.

Love at First Sight?

When Henry VIII met Anne of Cleves for the first time, at Rochester on New Year's Day 1540, he was so shaken by her appearance, which bore scant resemblance to the picture of her that had induced him to agree to the marriage in the first place, that he completely forgot to present her with the engagement gift he had brought with him.

Love, Honour and Obey

Catherine Parr, Henry VIII's sixth and last wife, already knew something of married life (and older husbands) when she accepted the king's hand in marriage. As a 14-year-old, she had been married off by her widowed mother to Edward de Burgh, second Baron Borough of Gainsborough in Lincolnshire. He was around 63 at the time and old enough to be Catherine's grandfather. Catherine became stepmother to his children, who themselves were old enough to be her parents. Among the family, the closest to her in age were her husband's grandchildren by his son and heir, Thomas de Burgh, who was 38 at the time of her marriage.

Lust is Blind

Within a short time of his marriage to Catherine Howard it became evident that Henry's pretty young queen was also promiscuous. However, during the brief period of his infatuation with her, Henry famously described Catherine Howard as a 'rose without a thorn'.

Maintaining the Royal Line

As Henry VIII's sixth wife and queen, Catherine Parr took care to get on well with her stepchildren and it was probably thanks to her that the king's daughters, Mary and Elizabeth, were again added to the line of royal succession in the Act of Succession that was passed in February 1544. In fact, Queen Catherine had begged her husband to allow Lady Mary to follow in succession to her brother, Prince Edward. But Henry was adamant that any children born to him and Catherine should take precedence over Mary, and of course over Elizabeth.

Mark of a King

Henry's motto was *Coeur Loyal* (True Heart), which was embroidered on the king's clothes in the form of a heart symbol and the world 'loyal'.

Marriage Lines

Bluff Henry the Eighth to six spouses was wedded:
One died, one survived, two divorced, two beheaded.

18th-century nursery rhyme

May Day

Many of the rites that had their roots in pagan fertility festivals survived in the 16th century as May Day traditions, which made 1 May one of the great holidays of the year.

Both Henry VIII and Catherine of Aragon joined in the festivities and went 'a-Maying' with as much enthusiasm as their courtiers and members of the royal household. Early 'on the morn of May' they went 'into the woods and meadows to divert themselves' and then took part in traditional games and maypole dancing. On May Day 1510 it was reported that, 'His Grace, being young and not willing to be idle, rose very early to fetch in the may and green boughs, himself fresh and richly apparelled, and all his knights in white satin … and went every man with his bow and arrows shooting in the wood, and so returned to court, every man with a green bough in his cap.'

Meanwhile the ladies were busy gathering dew in the early hours of May-morning, in order to wash their faces in it. It was an ancient belief that May dew had the power to make complexions beautiful, to remove freckles and other blemishes, and to bring good luck for the coming 12 months.

Catherine of Aragon evidently set great store by it and there is at least one account that on May Day 1515 she and 25 of her ladies went dew-gathering in the early hours, when it could be collected from the grass and bushes, in order to anoint their faces.

Mid-Life Vices

'This Prince seems tainted with three vices: the first is that he is so covetous that all the riches of the world would not satisfy him. Thence proceeds the second, distrust and fear. This King, knowing how many changes he has made, and what tragedies and scandals he has created, would fain keep in favour with everybody, but does not trust a single man, expecting to see them all offended, and he will not cease to dip his hand in blood as long as he doubts his people. The third vice [is] lightness and inconstancy.'

Charles de Marillac, the French ambassador, on the middle-aged Henry VIII

Missing Son

In addition to the legitimate children who survived him, there is a suggestion that Henry VIII fathered an illegitimate child, Henry Fitzroy, by his mistress Elizabeth (Bessie) Blount. Although he was never officially acknowledged by Henry, young Fitzroy was made Duke of Richmond in June 1525 – an act that some saw as a move towards legitimising him. However, this did not happen and Henry Fitzroy never became king. In 1536, three years after marrying Mary Howard, Henry Fitzroy died leaving no successors to pursue a claim to the English crown.

Mistaken Identity

In his *Book of Martyrs* John Foxe (1516–87) describes how Catholic intriguers planned the overthrow of Henry VIII's sixth wife and Protestant sympathiser, Catherine Parr, and that the king actually signed a warrant without realising it. The king and queen were walking in the garden at Hampton Court when a party of 40 royal guards, led by the then lord chancellor (Sir Thomas Wriothesley), arrived to arrest her. The king took the chancellor aside and exchanged some heated words with him: including outbursts of 'Knave!', 'Beast!' and 'Fool!'

In the end Queen Catherine tried to intercede for the chancellor, only to be told by her husband, 'Ah! Poor soul. Thou little knowest how ill he deserveth this at thy hands. On my word, sweetheart, he hath been to thee a very knave.'

The Morning After

'I repayring to your Majesty into your prevy Chambre Fynding your grace not as pleasaunte as I trustyd to have done I was so bolde as to aske your grace how he lykd the queen Whereunto your grace Sobyrly answeryd saying That I was not all men Surelye my lord as ye know. I likyd her her beffor not well but now I lyke her moche worse For quoth your highness I haue Felte her belye and her breasts and therby, as I can Judge She Sholde be noe Mayde which strake me so to the harte when I Felt that that I hadde nother will nor Corage to procede any ferther in other matyrs, saying I have left her as good a mayde as I founde her.'

Letter from Thomas Cromwell to Henry VIII, in June 1540, reminding Henry of his words to Cromwell, after his wedding night with Anne of Cleves, which had proved to be as much of a disappointment as his new bride's physical appearance

Mother Figure

Alhough Henry VIII was fond of his children, he remained distant and intimidating. All three had lost their mothers, although Elizabeth and Edward had been too young to remember theirs; so the arrival in their lives of the kind and caring Catherine Parr as Henry VIII's sixth and last wife brought reassurance and a degree of reunion with their father.

Catherine was only four years older that Princess Mary and had already made her a close friend. It was Catherine who made it possible for Mary to come to court more often than she had at any time in her life. Catherine was equally at ease acting as a substitute mother for Henry's two younger children. Thanks to her, Elizabeth was allocated lodgings in royal palaces for the first time in her life. Though Edward was generally kept away from court, living in his own household which was deemed by his father to be safer for his health, Catherine occasionally arranged for all three children to join her and the king when they were visiting one of the minor royal houses.

Musical Diversions

Among his collection of musical instruments, Henry VIII counted 26 lutes, along with trumpets, viols, rebecs, sackbuts, fifes, drums, harpsichords and organs. Henry is said to have played the lute well, to have been proficient at the organ and to have played the virginals with skill.

New Year's Day

In Henry VIII's time it was customary to give presents during the Christmas period, but not on Christmas Day. Tudor presents were exchanged on New Year's Day and in the case of the king this took place in a glittering ceremony where, as well as the queen and the royal family, every courtier and servant gave the king a gift, each of which was carefully noted down on an official roll before being displayed for everyone to admire.

Gold, sliver plate, jewellery and money formed the majority of the royal gifts, though wealthy nobles vied with each other to give Henry the most valuable and novel presents: Cardinal Wolsey was in the habit of giving his sovereign a gold cup worth over £30,000 in today's money.

In return, Henry presented every member of the royal household with gifts of plate, such as cups and bowls, engraved with his royal cipher and each one sized strictly according to the rank and status of the recipient.

Not in Front of the King

In spite of his reputation for boisterous entertainment and the evident enthusiasm with which he pursued women, Henry VIII was offended by vulgar language and bawdy humour. On one occasion, while he was travelling by barge to Greenwich Tower to visit 'a fair lady whom he loved and lodged in the tower of the park', the king was 'disposed to be merry' and invited one of his companions, Sir Andrew Flammock, to complete a rhyme for him.

The king supplied the first three lines, which he had composed himself:

Within this tower
There lieth a flower
That hath my heart …

Now it was Sir Andrew's turn, and he offered the following:

Within this hour
She pissed full sour
And let a fart

This was certainly not what the king had expected and in his outrage he exclaimed 'Begone, varlet!' and waved the foul-mouthed courtier from his sight.

Off With Our Heads

'Alas, it pitieth me to think into what misery she will shortly come. Those dances of hers will spin off our heads like footballs, but it will not be long ere she will dance headless.'

Sir Thomas More on Anne Boleyn, in 1532. Four years later he was proved right, although by then More himself had been executed.

Off With Their Heads

According to the 16th-century English chronicler Raphael Holinshed, 72,000 people were executed during Henry VIII's 38-year reign. If that is true, the execution rate during his time on the throne exceeded an average of five a day.

On His Majesty's Service

Catherine Parr, who had become a bride at 14, was a widow at 16 following the death of her 65-year-old husband, Lord Borough, in 1529. The following year her mother died leaving Catherine a not inconsiderable fortune, and it wasn't long after that she married for a second time, becoming the third wife of John Neville, Lord Latimer. Catherine remained Lady Latimer for 14 years until her husband's death in March 1543. His estates, combined with her mother's inheritance, made Catherine a woman of great means.

However, King Henry was not the only man at court with an interest in the widowed Lady Latimer. At 31 she entered into a flirtation with Sir Thomas Seymour, the dashing 37-year-old brother of the late Queen Jane and uncle to the heir to the throne, Prince Edward. Before long, Catherine had fallen in love with Seymour and the two of them had begun to discuss marriage. But Henry had other ideas and removed his rival by sending Seymour to Brussels on a permanent embassy. That was in May 1543. By the summer of that year it was clear that marriage with Seymour was out of the question (as long as Henry was alive) so when the king proposed to her she accepted and the couple were married on 12 July at Hampton Court.

Pain of Rejection

Catherine of Aragon suffered the pain and humiliation of a discarded and unwanted wife, after Henry tired of her and sought to replace her with Anne Boleyn. In November 1531, she wrote to the Emperor Charles V, 'My tribulations are so great, my life so disturbed by the plans daily invented to further the king's wicked intention, the surprises which the king gives me, with certain persons of his council, are so mortal, and my treatment is what God knows, that it is enough to shorten ten lives, much more mine.'

In another account she is quoted as saying, 'In this world I will confess myself to be the king's true wife, and in the next they will know how unreasonably I am afflicted.'

Paternal Pride

Henry VIII regarded hunting as a suitable education for a gentleman. 'It behoves the sons of gentlemen to blow horn calls correctly, to hunt skillfully, to train a hawk well and carry it elegantly,' wrote an anonymous subject, and Henry took a close interest in his own children's exploits in the hunting field.

In 1525 he was told that his young son, the illegitimate Henry Fitzroy the Duke of Richmond, although ill and being carried in a litter for several miles, had shot a deer by himself in Clyff Park in Northamptonshire. This would have been impressive for anyone feeling as unwell as he was, but as the boy was only six years old the account of his achievement was clearly meant to impress his father.

Pearls ~~Before~~ Swine

In 1545 Henry VIII moved to restrict the reading of the Bible to noble men and women, even though it was now available in English translations. Addressing Parliament on the subject, the king announced '... although you be permitted to read Holy Scripture and to have the Word of God in your mother-tongue, you must understand that it is licensed you so to do only to inform your own conscience and to instruct your children and family ... I am very sorry to know and hear how unreverently that most precious jewel, the Word of God, is disputed, rhymed, sung and jangled in every ale-house and tavern, contrary to the true meaning and doctrine of the same.'

People's Favourite

Henry's first wife, Catherine of Aragon, was described as 'rather ugly than otherwise; of low stature and rather stout; very good and very religious; speaks Spanish, French, Flemish, English; more beloved by the islanders than any queen that has ever reigned'.

Personal Hygiene

Elizabeth I was celebrated for her obsession with cleanliness, taking a bath at least once a month 'whether she needed it or no'. This was a characteristic that she shared with her father, who was fastidious in his attempts to banish dirt, dust and smells from his immediate environment. Royal edicts were regularly issued to enforce the king's strict hygiene wherever he was staying, but in an age of primitive sanitation these were hard to enforce. Servants that came into close contact with the king were obliged above all others to keep themelves wholesome. The king's barber was required to ensure that he was 'pure and clean' at all times; he was also instructed to keep away from 'vile persons' and to have nothing to do with 'misguided women'.

One of the reasons he gave for not consummating his marriage to Anne of Cleves was that he could not abide the stench of her body odour.

Playing for the Highest Stakes

'At the opening of the year 1536 Anne Boleyn's position rested on two supports: the life of Catherine of Aragon and the prospect of a prince. Never was fortune more cruel. On January 7th Catherine died, and on the twenty-ninth, the day of the funeral, Anne gave premature birth to a male child. She had miscarried of her saviour. The tragedy must obviously move to a close; and it moved swiftly. On May 2nd she was arrested and sent to the tower, accused of adultery with five men, one of whom was her brother. In the subsequent trials all were found guilty, and the law took its course. Anne herself was executed on May 18th. Whether she was guilty or not, no human judgement can now determine, and contemporaries differed. In all probability she had been indiscreet. If she had gone further, if she had really committed adultery – and that possibility cannot be lightly dismissed – then it is likely that a desperate woman had taken a desperate course to give England its prince and save herself from ruin. Whatever the truth, she had played her game and lost.'

J E Neale, *Queen Elizabeth*

Pox on the King

'Item, that he, having the French pox, presumed to come and breathe on the king.'

From *The Articles of Parliament Against Wolsey*, 1529, which laid charges against the cardinal that led to his impeachment and execution

Prayers and Promises

The library at Alnwick Castle in Northumberland has Anne Boleyn's prayer book, inscribed with her motto 'The most happy'.

Pretended Matrimony

Henry VIII found disposing of his fourth wife, Anne of Cleves, considerably easier than any of the previous three.

Anne of Cleves behaved with dignity and agreed to the annulment of her marriage without fuss. As a result, she was allowed to remain in

England as a wealthy dowager and made periodic visits to court with her ex-husband's full approval:

'... though it be determined that the pretended matrimony between us is void and of none effect, whereby I neither can nor will repute myself for your grace's wife, considering this sentence (whereunto I stand) and your majesty's clean and pure living with me, yet it will please you to take me for one of your humble servants, and so determine of me, as I may sometimes have the fruition of your most noble presence; which as I shall esteem for a great benefit, so, my lords and others of your majesty's council, now being with me, have put me in comfort thereof; and that your highness will take me for your sister; for the which I most humbly thank you accordingly.

Thus, most gracious prince, I beseech our Lord God to send your majesty long life and good health, to God's glory, your own honour, and the wealth of this noble realm.

From Richmond, the 11th day of July, the 32nd year of your majesty's most noble reign [1540].

Your majesty's most humble sister and servant, Anne the daughter of Cleves.'

The Prince and the Poet

As a young man Henry VIII counted the poet John Skelton among his tutors.

A Prince at Play

Passetyme in good companye
I love and shall unto I dye,
Gruche so wylle,
But none deny,
So God plecyd, so lyf woll I.
For my pastaunce
Hunte, syng & daunce,
My hert is sett:
All godely sport
To my comfort
Who shal me lett?

Henry VIII on himself, printed in Horace Walpole's
Catalogue of Royal and Noble Authors

Princely Perversity

The average life expectancy for Tudor men was 45 and although Henry VIII was deemed to be in reasonable physical health for a man of his age, the stress and demands of kingship had taken their toll on his personality. The once liberal, idealistic young king had been replaced by a dogmatic, unpredictable autocrat. The ambassador of the Holy Roman Empire, Eustace Chapuys, expressed the widely held opinion of the king's change in character when he commented, 'Such are the King's fickleness and natural inclination to new or strange things that I could not find words to describe it. His natural inclination is to oppose all things debatable, taking great pride in persuading himself that he makes the world believe one thing instead of another.'

Prophetic Judgement

'God has given you great qualities. Cultivate them always, and labour to improve them, for I believe you are destined by Heaven to be Queen of England.'

Words reputedly spoken by Catherine Parr to her stepdaughter Princess Elizabeth, in May 1547

67

Pursuit of Knowledge

Unlike his father, Henry VIII found writing 'both tedious and painful'. He was not a natural scholar, but he had an enquiring mind. In his more civilised moments he spent time studying theology and astronomy.

His was a restless pursuit of knowledge, however. Sir Thomas More's biographer and son-in-law, Sir William Roper, records that the king was in the habit of taking More 'into his private room, and there some time in matters of astronomy, geometry, divinity and such other faculties, and some time in his worldly affairs, to sit and confer with him, and other whiles would he in the night have him up on the leads [the roof] there to consider with him the diversities, courses, motions and operations of the stars and planets.'

The Queen is Dead ... Long Live the Queen

On the morning of Anne Boleyn's execution, Henry was out hunting and as soon as the boom of the gun signalling his second wife's death reached him, he shouted gleefully, 'Uncouple the hounds, and away!'

Leaving the hunt to pursue whatever game they could find, Henry and his courtiers galloped at full speed to Wolf Hall, Jane Seymour's maternal home, where she had retired from court while Henry was disposing of his most recent wife. The king's party reached Wolf Hall by nightfall and early the following morning, dressed as a bridegroom, he led Jane Seymour to the altar and made her his third bride. From there the happy couple made a leisurely return to London over the next nine days, at the end of which Jane Seymour was introduced as queen before feasts, jousts and other entertainments were staged in honour of the latest royal wedding.

The Rarest Man

Henry VIII's earliest biographer was William Thomas, who set to work on his account of the late monarch's life in 1547, the year Henry died. For someone writing so close to the reign that had just ended, Thomas's opinion of his royal master makes an interesting counterpoint to the harsher judgements of historians who came after him (notably Sir Walter Raleigh whose own opinion is expressed later). Henry VIII, Thomas asserted, 'was undoubtedly the rarest man living in his time. I say not this to make him a god, nor in all his doings I will not say he has been a saint. He did many evil things, but not as a cruel tyrant or as a hypocrite. I wot not where in all the histories I have read to find one king equal to him.'

Rebellious Subjects

In autumn of 1536 Henry VIII's moves to seize Church property combined with growing resentment at tax increases and boiled over in an uprising in Lincolnshire. This uprising was crushed by the king, who led a force of 5,000 men to suppress the rebels. When all resistance and dissent had been stamped out, a furious Henry delivered this warning to his cowed subjects:

'How presumptuous then are ye, the rude commons of one shire ... to find fault with your Prince ... Wherefore, Sirs, remember your follies and traitorous demeanours, and shame not your undoubted King and natural Prince ...; and remember your duty of allegiance, and that ye are bound to obey us, your King, both by God's commandment and law of nature ... Withdraw yourselves to your own houses, every man; and no more assemble, contrary to our laws and your allegiances; ... or put yourselves, your lives and wives, children, lands, goods and chattels, besides the indignation of God, in the utter adventure of total destruction and utter ruin by force and violence of the sword.'

In the event of any further rising, Henry ordered the Duke of Suffolk immediately to attack Louth and 'with all extremity destroy, burn and kill, man, woman, and child, for the terrible example of all others'.

Richmond Palace

Described by a contemporary commentator as 'an earthly paradise, most glorious to behold', Richmond Palace was regarded as Henry VIII's masterpiece.

Henry had his palace constructed of red brick and stone on the ruins of the old medieval palace of Sheen, which had been burned to the ground in 1497. Rebuilt on a courtyard plan with huge bay windows, fairy-tale pinnacles and turrets surmounted by bell-shaped domes and gilded weather-vanes, the new palace was renamed Richmond, by royal decree, after the earldom held by Henry VIII's father before he became King Henry VII.

Richmond Palace had fountains in the courtyards, orchards and 'most fair and pleasant gardens' laid out in a formal Renaissance pattern and intersected by wide paths and statues of the king's beasts. Running around the gardens were two-storey, galleried timber-framed walks.

The royal lodgings were housed in a central tower, or donjon, built of stone. Inside, the beamed ceilings were painted azure and studded with gold Tudor roses and portcullises. The walls were decorated with rich tapestries, portraits and murals painted by Henry VII's court artist, Maynard the Fleming. These depicted 'the noble kings of this realm in harness and robes of gold, as Brutus, Hengist, King William Rufus, King Arthur [and] King Henry … with swords in their hands, appearing like bold and valiant knights'. Henry VII had also created a richly appointed chapel and a well-stocked library, inherited by his son.

The whole complex was surrounded by a 'mighty brick wall' with a tower at each corner. At the centre stood the main gate made of 'double timber and heart of oak, studded full of nails and crossed with bars of iron'. Above it were mounted the arms of Henry VII, supported by the red dragon of Wales and the greyhound of Richmond.

If any single building symbolised the spirit of the new Tudor dynasty, it was Richmond Palace.

Room for Reflection

The night before her execution Anne Boleyn was held in the room in the Tower of London where she had stayed the night before her coronation.

Rough Wooing

The so-called 'rough wooing' was the period beginning May 1544 when Henry VIII gave up further attempts to win round the people of Scotland through peaceful diplomacy. Instead his forces were ordered to follow a policy of ruthless military devastation, during which crops were burned and Edinburgh and Leith were sacked.

Royal Accommodation

In the early years of Henry's reign, before the dissolution of the monasteries, he often stayed in monastic guest houses or apartments especially reserved for him. Elsewhere, he would lodge with one of his courtiers or a member of the local nobility, who was expected to give way to the king, allowing him to become lord of the house for the duration of his stay. With the king in residence, his apartments in the house became a temporary royal chamber at court, and his attendants and servants were expected to take priority over those of his host.

The knight harbinger was responsible for allocating accommodation following a strict order of precedence, in which those closest to the king occupied the rooms in the house nearest his. Before the royal party arrived, a gentleman usher was sent ahead to check that their destination satisfied the basic criteria for accommodating the king and his retinue: in other words that it had a sound roof and walls, and that the doors were all fitted with locks.

Some houses, of course, were not large enough to accommodate such a sizeable influx of visitors. In these circumstances, barns and stables were taken over and tents were erected in the grounds.

Royal Duties

When he was five years old, the Duke of York, as the future Henry VIII was then styled, carried out what was probably his first public act, when he witnessed a royal grant by charter to the abbot and convent of Glastonbury in Somerset to hold two annual fairs. Forty-three years later Henry had reduced the Glastonbury Abbey to ruins and had ordered its last abbot to be hanged for treason on the Tor, which looks over the abbey site.

Royal Navy

Henry VIII is traditionally referred to as one of the founders of the Royal Navy. During his reign there was a large investment in shipbuilding, dock-yards and naval warfare – including the arming of naval vessels with cannon. Some tactics remained unchanged, however and Henry's ships were still manned with companies of archers firing arrows from the fore-castle as their medieval forebears had for several centuries.

Royal Progress

Almost every year of his reign Henry VIII visited different parts of his realm in an extended journey, or progress, between July and October. This gave him the chance to see and be seen by his subjects; it also enabled him to enjoy the hunting (his hunting dogs travelled with him, transported by cart) and hospitality available throughout the country.

Henry was accompanied by a small retinue of courtiers, sometimes by his riding household alone, though the queen usually travelled with him. The chapel royal, travelling with him wherever he went, had the dual role of conducting religious services and providing musical entertainment.

Royal Record-Breaker

Queen Catherine Parr was the only one of the six wives of Henry VIII to outlive him; she was also England's most-married queen.

Royal Relations

Although Henry pretended that his third wife and queen, Jane Seymour, had descended, through her mother, from the royal line of England, few with any knowledge of genealogy accepted this. In marrying Jane, Henry acquired a brother-in-law with the surname Smith and another whose grandfather was a blacksmith in Putney.

Royal Residences

By the end of Henry VIII's reign, there were 55 royal palaces.

A Royal Robin Hood

In his youth, Henry VIII was an accomplished sportsman. He could ride for hours on end, reputedly tiring eight or ten horses before tiring himself. He was a fine player of real (or royal) tennis. He carried away many prizes for jousting and tilting and his skill as an archer was outstanding, even in a nation famed for its archers.

The young king was said to be able to draw a long bow with greater strength than any man in England. On his first campaign at Calais in the summer of 1513, he joined the archers of the royal guard in archery practice and 'cleft the mark in the middle and surpassed them all, as he surpasses them in stature and personal graces'.

Scandalmongers Beware

The following love letter from Henry VIII to Jane Seymour is believed to have been written while Anne Boleyn was incarcerated in the Tower of London awaiting her execution. As well as expressing his strong affection for the woman who would soon become his next wife, Henry offers a dark warning to anyone taking the king's name in vain.

'My Dear friend and mistress,

The bearer of these few lines from thy entirely devoted servant will deliver into thy fair hands a token of my true affection for thee, hoping you will keep it for ever in your sincere love for me. Advertising you that there is a ballad made lately of great derision against us, which if it go abroad and is seen by you; I pray you to pay no manner of regard to it. I am not at present informed who is the setter forth of this malignant writing; but if he is found out, he shall be straitly punished for it.

For the things ye lacked, I have minded my lord to supply them to you as soon as he could buy them. Thus hoping, shortly to receive you in these arms, I end for the present,

Your own loving servant and sovereign.'

The Scholar Queen

Bright and intelligent herself, Catherine Parr was charged by Henry VIII to encourage and supervise the education of his two youngest children: Edward and Elizabeth. This was a task that his sixth wife acquitted admirably. Both children studied the classics, as well as music and religion. Princess Elizabeth received tuition in needlepoint and dance, as befitted a young lady of her status; her brother, meanwhile, developed his skill as a swordsman. Queen Catherine led by example and kept up her own course of studies. In November 1545, she published *Prayers and Meditations*, which she had collected and edited. Both universities at Oxford and Cambridge were so impressed by her work that they petitioned the queen to become their patroness; she accepted both invitations. At the same time she assisted the education of many poor students by paying their fees at Stoke College and by ensuring that all the children of her tenant farmers were schooled at her own expense.

Setting the Record Straight

For the official record, Henry VIII was only married twice. Since four of his marriages were annulled, technically they never took place.

Sex Appeal

'… not one of the handsomest women in the world. She is of middling stature, with a swarthy complexion, long neck, wide mouth, bosom not much raised, and in fact has nothing but the King's great appetite, and her eyes, which are black and beautiful – and take great effect … She lives like a Queen and the King accompanies her to Mass – and everywhere.'

The Venetian Ambassador on Anne Boleyn, in 1532, a year before her marriage to Henry VIII

Son and Heir

The question of providing a son and heir to carry forward the Tudor dynasty, founded by his father Henry VII, coloured much of Henry VIII's public and private life.

In his first marriage to Catherine of Aragon, the news that she was pregnant started him on a period of feverish preparation as he eagerly anticipated the birth. The king ordered a new cover for the font in which his longed-for baby son would be baptised, and commissioned special linen towels to dry the child. The royal nursery was similarly refurbished with a sumptuous cradle padded with crimson cloth of gold embroidered with the royal arms, and swaddling bands in which to wrap the infant. The nurses were provided with new beds. Two new rocking chairs were installed. New linen was bought for Queen Catherine's bed and a 'groaning chair' was commissioned, with a cut-away seat and upholstered in cloth of gold.

However, all these careful preparations and the air of expectancy only served to heighten the bitter disappointment that was to come. After an agonising labour, Catherine of Aragon was delivered of a stillborn daughter. No public announcement broadcast this crushing news and it took Catherine four months before she felt able to write to her father, King Ferdinand, to tell him of her loss.

A later pregnancy saw the successful birth of Princess Mary. But the disappointment of failing to sire a living son and heir was to dog Henry VIII time and again.

The Spirit of Sherwood Forest

In his younger days, Henry VIII was partial to playing tricks on the royal household and in January 1510 he staged the first of what would become known as his 'disguisings'. Early one morning, the king and 11 companions dressed themselves in short green coats and hoods to conceal their faces and, armed with bows and arrows, swords and bucklers, they stormed into the queen's chamber, greatly to the alarm of Catherine of Aragon and her ladies, who were described as being much 'abashed'. However, they regained their composure and agreed to dance with their visitors, who only revealed themselves when the dancing had ended and they threw back their hoods to disclose the king and his fellows – to their great amusement and the astonishment of the royal ladies.

Sport of Kings

Although the establishment of horse racing as we know it would have to wait another century and a half after the reign of Henry VIII, the king was as interested in fine bloodstock as his successors. His royal stables housed up to 200 horses, among them thoroughbreds imported from Europe at enormous expense. In 1509, the year in which she and Henry were married, Catherine of Aragon wrote to her father asking him to 'send to the King my lord three horses, one a jennet [a small Spanish riding horse], the other from Naples [Henry was particularly keen on light-footed Neapolitan coursers], and the other a Sicilian, because he desires them much, and has asked me to beg Your Highness for them, and also to command them to be sent by the first messenger that comes here'.

Sugar Daddy

Henry VIII was 49 when he married Catherine Howard at the end of July 1540, some 30 years older than his frivolous, flighty young bride, and by his own admission entered upon his old age. Even so, the king was described as being 'so amorous of her that he knows not how to make sufficient demonstrations of his affection, and caresses her more than he did the others'.

If the king was short of ideas on how to demonstrate his 'affections', Catherine was not. As another observer remarked, 'the King had no wife who made him spend so much money in dresses and jewels as she did, and every day some fresh caprice'.

It was reported that Catherine appeared every morning wearing a new gown. To keep her hands warm, the king gave her a sable-lined black velvet muff suspended from her neck by a gold and pearl chain. Tiny gold chains and hundreds of pearls and rubies decorated the muff itself. And this was just one of a seemingly inexhaustible supply of fabulous gifts that Henry lavished on Catherine Howard. Ropes of pearls, heavy gold chains, a gold brooch with scenes from the life of Noah picked out in diamonds, and crosses encrusted with precious stones joined a succession of costly ornaments in his young wife's jewellery box.

The Sum of All Evils

'… If all the pictures & patterns of a merciless prince were lost in the world, they might all again be painted to the life, out of the story of this King. For how many servants did he advance in haste (but for what virtue no man could suspect) and with the change of his fancy ruined again, no man knowing for what offence. To how many others of more desert gave he abundant flowers, from whence to gather honey and in the end of harvest burned them in the hive?'

Sir Walter Raleigh on Henry VIII, in his work *The Historie of the World*

Sweet Nothings

Researchers investigating Henry VIII's library discovered a number of secret love notes exchanged between Henry and Anne Boleyn scribbled in the margins of books.

Henry wrote, in French, in a 16th-century book of hours, 'If you remember me according to my love in your prayers I shall scarcely be forgotten, since I am your Henry Rex for ever.'

To this, Anne replied in doggerel verse:

Be daly prove you shall me fynde
To be to you bothe lovynge and kynde.

Thrill of the Chase

'The reasonable request of your last letter, with the pleasure also that I take to know them true, causeth me to send you these news. The legate whom we most desire arrived at Paris on Sunday or Monday last past, so that I trust by the next Monday to hear of his arrival at Calais; and then I trust within awhile after to enjoy that which I have so long longed for, to God's pleasure, and both our comforts.

No more to you at this present, mine own darling, for lack of time, but that I would you were in mine arms, or I in yours, for I think it long since I kissed you.

Written after the killing of a hart, at eleven of the clock, minding [intending], with God's grace, to-morrow, mighty timely, to kill another, by the hand which, I trust, shortly shall be yours,

HENRY R'

Letter from Henry VIII to Anne Boleyn, believed to date from 1527

After Jane Seymour went into labour with her son, Prince Edward, her condition worsened significantly and the physicians attending her feared for her life. They asked the king which he wished to be saved: the mother or the child.

Henry's reply was characteristically ruthless. 'If you cannot save both, at least let the child live,' he told them, 'for other wives are easily found.'

Tilting and Tournaments

Tournaments in the medieval tradition were still enormously popular in the reign of Henry VIII, largely because the king was a keen and successful participant and because he saw tournaments providing 'honourable and healthy exercise' that kept aristocratic fighting men in peak condition.

Such displays of 'martial feats' also became opulent social events in which the king and his nobles could display their wealth and prowess before a large audience, including influential visitors from abroad. Under Henry's patronage, tournaments held in England became renowned throughout Europe for their lavish spectacle and the skill of those competing.

Tournaments were often held over several days and provided the principal entertainment at court festivals and state visits. There were also regular tournaments through the months of May and June before the beginning of the hunting season. Contests took the form of different kinds of armed combat. There was hand-to-hand fighting on foot with a range of weapons. Contestants at the 'barriers' fought opponents with swords across a waist-high wooden fence. Mounted on horseback, knights fought each other with swords in the tourney, and galloped towards each other with levelled lances either side of a wooden palisade in the tilt (when competitors fought in pairs) or the joist (when they fought alone).

Jousting called for strength, a good aim and a fine sense of timing if serious injury or death were to be avoided. Success in the joist carried almost as much prestige as achieving glory on the battlefield.

Marks were awarded depending on the parts of an opponent's armour that were hit. A blow to the helmet scored the highest mark, closely followed by one struck on the breastplate. When competing in the tilt, the objective was to unseat an opponent, or split his lance.

Trial and Punishment

'This year [1541] on 13 November Sir Thomas Wriothesley, secretary to the king, came to Hampton Court to the queen, and called all the ladies and gentlewomen and her servants into the great chamber, and there openly before them declared certain offences she had committed in misusing her body with certain persons before the king's time, because of which he there discharged all her household; …

On 1 December Thomas Culpepper, one of the gentlemen of the king's privy chamber, and Francis Dorand [Dereham], gentleman, were arraigned at the Guildhall in London, for high treason against the king's majesty, in misdemeanour with the queen, as appeared by their indictment which they confessed to, and they were sentenced to be drawn, hanged, and quartered … And on 10 December the said Culpepper and Dorand were drawn from the Tower of London to Tyburn, and there Culpepper, after exhorting the people to pray for him, stood on the ground by the gallows, knelt down and had his head struck off; and then Dorand was hanged, dismembered, disemboweled, beheaded and quartered. Culpepper's body was buried at St Sepulchre's church near Newgate, and their heads were set on London Bridge [where they remained until at least 1546].'

The Spanish ambassador, Eustace Chapuys, recording the fall of Catherine Howard and the two men with whom she was accused of 'misdemeanour'. Two months later Catherine herself was executed, on 13 February 1542.

A Tudor Rose

The 30 years of civil war fought in England in the second half of the 15th century became known as the Wars of the Roses because of the emblems of the rival factions: the white rose of York and the red rose of Lancaster. With his victory at the Battle of Bosworth in 1485, Henry VIII's father, Henry Tudor (head of the house of Lancaster), brought the Wars of the Roses to an end. He became Henry VII and in 1486 married princess Elizabeth of York. This union of the two houses was symbolised in the Tudor rose, in which the white rose is superimposed over the red.

For the contemporary poet John Skelton, Henry VIII personified the best qualities of this royal reconciliation, as expressed in his poem 'A Laud and Praise Made for Our Sovereign Lord the King':

The Rose both White and Red
In one Rose now doth grow:
Thus through every sted
Thereof the fame doth blow.
Grace the seed did sow:
England, now all floures,
Exclude now all doloures.

United in Death

When Henry VIII died he was buried, at his request, in the tomb in St George's Chapel, Windsor, where he had laid Jane Seymour to rest. She was the only one of his six wives to be buried with him.

The Verdict of History

'The plain truth is, that he was a most intolerable ruffian, a disgrace to human nature, and a blot of blood and grease upon the History of England.'
Charles Dickens on Henry VIII, in *A Child's History of England*

A Very Fleshly Man

Throughout his life Henry VIII was known to have more than a lecherous streak in his approach to women. Writing in 1533 the king's cousin, Reginald Pole, observed that when she refused to follow her sister into the king's bed, Anne Boleyn had wisely remembered 'how soon he was sated with those who had served him as his mistress'.

The royal physician, Dr John Chamber, more or less confirmed this in the medical parlance of his day when he described his royal patient as being 'overly fond of women' and given to 'lustful dreams'.

William Thomas, the author of a predominantly favourable biography of his royal master, written around the time of Henry's death, felt the need to state, 'it cannot be denied but that he was a very fleshly man, and no marvel, for albeit his father brought him up in good learning, yet after he fell into all riot and overmuch love of women'.

Cardinal Wolsey was accused by his enemies, of whom there were many, of acting as 'the King's bawd, showing him what women were most wholesome and best of complexions'.

While Wolsey, naturally, dismissed the accusation, there was no denying Henry's evident interest in members of the opposite sex. A later 16th-century Catholic commentator claimed that, 'King Henry gave his mind to three notorious vices – lechery, covetousness and cruelty, but the two latter issued and sprang out of the former.' And the Elizabethan courtier

Sir Robert Naunton voiced what was by then well known, when he stated that Henry never spared a man in his anger nor a woman in his lust.

Voices of Men and of Angels

Henry VIII was credited with a strong, sure singing voice and he took great care to recruit the best boy and men singers for his chapels royal. He had music wherever he went: on progress round the country, on military campaigns and at court. Renaissance sacred music was added to the repertoire of the royal chapel in 1516 and, in the words of an Italian visitor, the choir who sang it was 'more divine than human'.

The Weight of Kingship

As he grew older Henry became grossly overweight and his waist measurement grew to 137cm (54 inches). This increase in his girth was caused in part by a jousting wound in his thigh dating from 1536. This prevented him from taking further exercise, but also became ulcerated over time and may have contributed to his death a decade later. He also gained a significant amount of weight following the death of Jane Seymour. This was compounded by what was described as 'a marvellous excess' in eating and drinking, in which he indulged to take his mind off Catherine Howard when her betrayal and adultery was unmasked. Before long it was claimed that 'the King was so fat that three of the biggest men that could be found could get inside his doublet'.

So now all is gone. Empire, body, soul.

The last words of King Henry VIII